Hello dear children, these animals are confused and trying to remember their names. Help them with that and write them in the appropriate fields in front of them.

WORD LIST

- **DONKEY**
- Cow
- *camel*

WORD LIST

- SHEEP
- PIG
- ROOSTER

WORD LIST
DOG
GOAT
RABBIT

WORD LIST
•HORSE
•GOOSE
•DUCK

WORD LIST
I.   ROOSTER
II.   TURKEY
III. CAT

WORD LIST
DEER
BEE
GRASSHOPPER

WORD
LIST
PANDA
FISH
FOX

WORD LIST
- MOUSE
- Owl
- goat

....

....

....

WORD LIST

- OCTUBUS
- LION
- PARROT

WORD LIST
SNAKE
SPIDER
TURTLE

WORD LIST
SNAIL
SEAGULL
SKUN

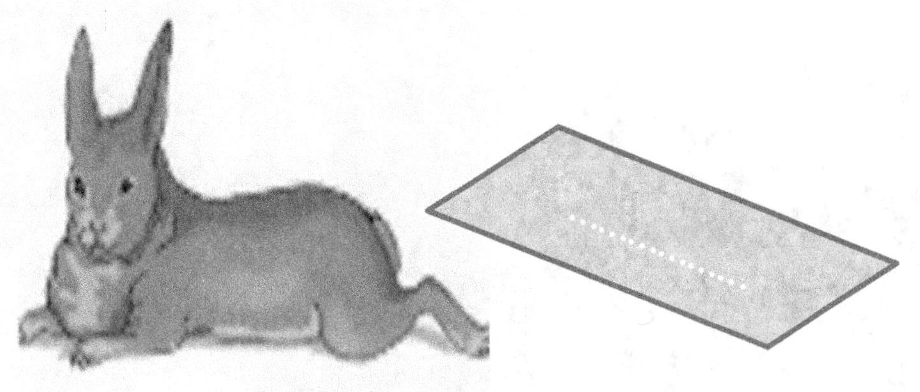

....

....

....

WORD LIST

WHALE

RHINO

RABBIT

Word list
Elephant
Tiger
denguin

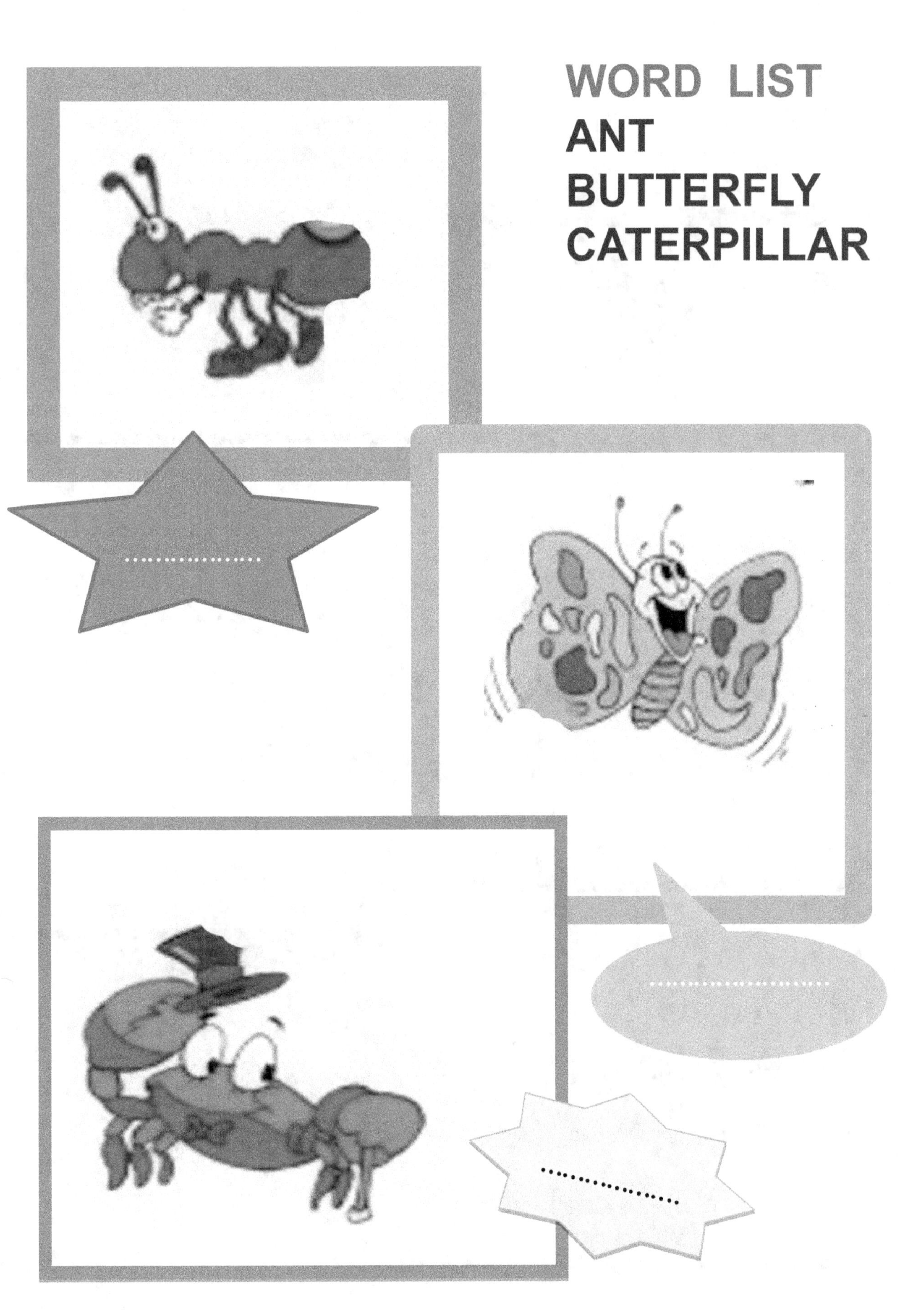
WORD LIST
ANT
BUTTERFLY
CATERPILLAR

WORD LIST
ANT
SHARK
CATERPILLAR

WORD LIST
BAT
BEAVER
BULL

WORD LIST
CHICKEN
KANGAROO
GIRAFFE

WORD LIST

VULTURE

SWORDFISH

CROCODILE

WORD LIST
ZEBRA
FROG
DONKEY

WORD LIST
SQUIRREL
BEAR

COW

Key
word

CAMEL

DONKEY

BIG
SHEEP
ROOSTER

RABBIT
GOAT
DOG

GOOSE
HORSE
DUCK

ROOSTER
CAT
TURKEY

Bee
Deer
Grasshopper

Fish
Fox
Bear

Mouse

Goat

Lion
Parrot
Octopus

Turtle
Snake
Spider

Snail

Skunk
Seagull

Rabbit

Rhino
Whale

Elephant
Tiger
Penguin

Ant

Butterfly

Caterpillar

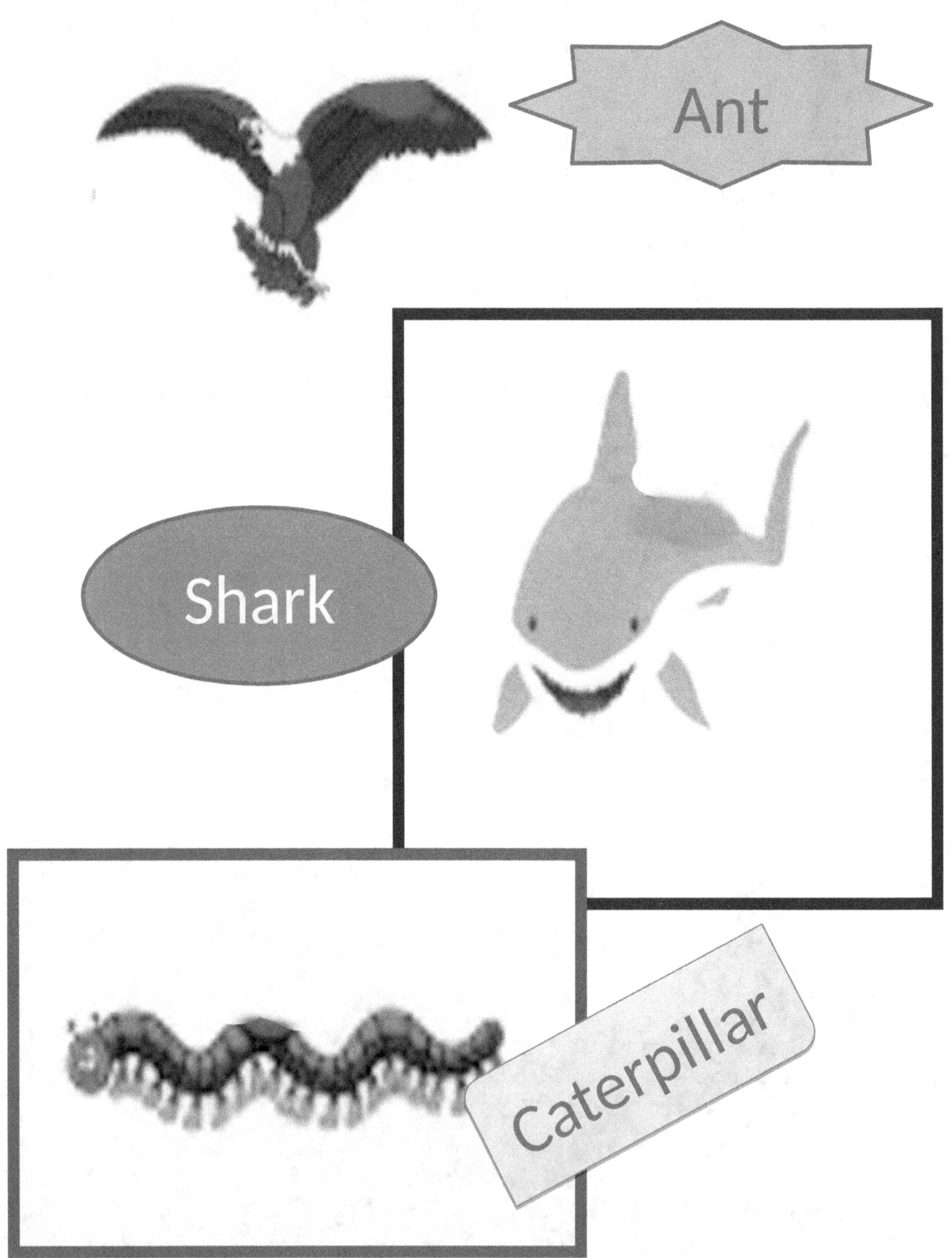

Ant
Shark
Caterpillar

Bat
Bull
Beaver

Kangaroo

chicke
n

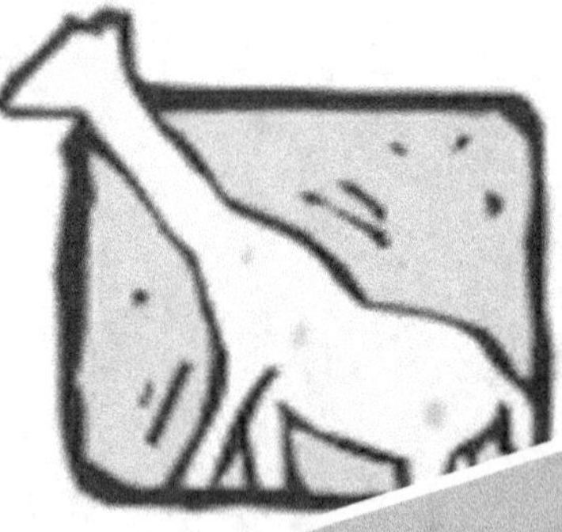

Giraffe

Crocodile
Vulture
Swordfish

Zebra
Monkey

Squirrel

Bear